THE ESSENTIAL BOOK OF
DRUIDRY

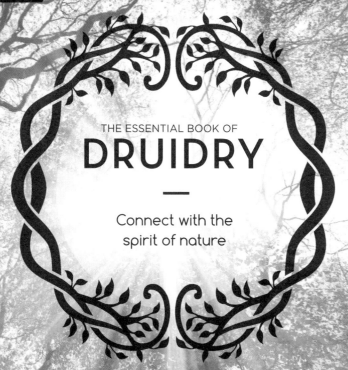

THE ESSENTIAL BOOK OF
DRUIDRY

—

Connect with the
spirit of nature

MARIA EDE-WEAVING

SIRIUS

For my father Bertie, who inspired in
me a deep love of nature, and
an appreciation of the wild paths,
where getting lost is the beginning
of finding your true home.

Images courtesy of Shutterstock.

SIRIUS

This edition published in 2023 by Sirius Publishing, a division of
Arcturus Publishing Limited,
26/27 Bickels Yard, 151–153 Bermondsey Street,
London SE1 3HA

ISBN: 978-1-3988-2618-2
AD010591UK

Printed in China

Contents

Introduction

Many years ago, I visited Cornwall for the Winter Solstice, staying in a slate cottage near Tintagel. A few days after the solstice, I woke at dawn to watch the sunrise. The sky was a wash of pastels but with a striking, vividly pink high bank of cloud coming in across the Atlantic.

As I stood awed by the beauty of the morning, I became aware of movement in my peripheral vision. Next to the cottage, in the herringbone pattern of a dry-stone wall, was a tiny wren. It hopped in and out of the gaps in the slate, finding tasty morsels of breakfast. As I became transfixed by this tiny bird, I felt with sudden clarity the answer to a dilemma I had been pondering. Having practised Wicca for some years, I was feeling curious about Druidry. I had briefly researched the training programme of the Order of Bards, Ovates and Druids and wondered if I should enroll and start my journey in earnest. For some reason, the appearance of that tiny bird felt like a message, and so began my Druid adventure. I did not know at that point that the wren was a sacred bird of Druidry and that its presence would act like a signpost on my path.

My stay in Cornwall, with its extraordinary landscape, brought many profound experiences. Local legend has it that Tintagel Castle was the birthplace of King Arthur, and beneath its steep cliffs Merlin's Cave runs like an underworld passage from one side of the island to the other. The north Cornish coast is steeped in myth and the land itself feels ancient and vibrantly alive.

My cottage overlooked St Nectan's Glen, a steep wooded valley with an unusual waterfall. Here the river drops down 60 feet into a stone bowl, or kieve, through which it has carved its way onwards creating a natural arch in the rocks. Some believe that St Nectan was not a man but the Celtic god Nechtan, husband to Boann, goddess of the River Boyne in Ireland. According to legend, Nechtan was the keeper of the Well of Segais, the mythological source of the Boyne and home to the Salmon of Wisdom — a creature from the Fenian Cycle of Irish mythology.

It's not difficult to sense the ancient gods at St Nectan's Glen: the unusual shape of the waterfall and the extraordinary beauty and atmosphere of the place feel deeply sacred. If you follow the river inland from the ocean's edge, past labyrinths carved into the rock face, meandering through a wood of gnarled oaks to the waterfall, there is a feeling of pilgrimage. It is as if the walker were taking that journey to seek and be nourished by the water's wisdom; to be healed and upheld by Boann's magic. I fell wholly

in love with this place and, even after I left, its atmosphere followed me home, infusing that first year of Druid study with a special kind of energy and focus.

What those first early steps on my Druid path taught me was that the landscape is alive with meaning and magic; that the natural world is a powerful teacher and that it can speak to us of lost belonging and yearning for reconnection. If we engage and listen deeply to its voice, it can guide us back to that sacred source — to that place of wisdom deep within us — where the salmon swims in crystal waters and the old gods offer their profound healing and transformation. Druidry re-enchants our vision of the world.

Many years later, I appreciate the significance of that little wren. She is still hopping in and out of the gaps of that dry-stone wall within me, exploring its dark crevices and bright surfaces, its mossy patterns and forms, encouraging me to do the same in my exploration of self. She is my search for the wisdom of nature and the mystery and sacredness of life. I offer the words that follow as a guiding wren on your journey home.

CHAPTER ONE

Ancient Wisdom
~ Modern
Perspectives

What is Druidry?

Have you ever woken when the world is still a collage of shadows and gone out into the woods? Have you felt the cold air moistening on your upper lip as your breath moves in and out in a familiar rhythm or noticed your senses reaching into the fullness of the dark? Have you felt your muscles tightening against the early chill or heard the crunch of your step on frosty mulch as the thin, burning line of the sun rising breaks the horizon?

Have you ever lain in bed at night listening to the barking call of a fox? Or watched a V of geese at sunset, or heard the mournful curlew sing its lament across the marsh flats? Or maybe you have walked down a busy city street, the sun flushing your cheeks and the thick heat rising from the paving, and spotted a lone wagtail speedily racing and weaving amongst the walkers?

Such experiences remind us that we exist in a material world but not a mundane one. They perhaps stir a memory within us from our childhoods when we were absorbed by the wonder around us — keen to explore its mysteries, curious and alive to every new discovery. We might recall from that time a deep sense

of belonging as we felt the grass between our toes and the wide sky arching protectively over us.

That memory of a carefree engagement with nature can feel particularly poignant in these troubled times. Humankind currently faces unprecedented challenges. We are confronted by a climate crisis. Our planet is increasingly rocked by extreme weather events that threaten human communities and delicate eco-systems, endangering the survival of countless species. It is now widely accepted that humans have accelerated these changes. We have reached a tipping point and are beginning to recognize ourselves as dysfunctional inhabitants of the planet we call home. To survive and prevent irreversible damage, global warming demands that we examine ourselves and change our behaviour.

In the light of this existential crisis, many are now turning to Earth-based spiritual paths and philosophies that offer a more harmonious and balanced interaction with nature. These paths ask that we re-evaluate not only our relationship with the Earth, but also how we live in our communities and perceive ourselves in the deepest sense. In recognizing how these three areas of self, community and nature are interconnected and interdependent, we might find solutions that will pull us back from the brink.

Industrial culture has been attempting to operate outside nature's laws, excessively consuming and exploiting natural resources. However, many who are concerned with the direction we are taking, are now drawing inspiration from modern indigenous cultures and our ancient ancestors, searching for more sustainable templates. There is a call to live within nature's boundaries — a growing understanding that working in harmony with its delicate balance will aid not only our survival but our ability to function and flourish as humans. Druidry hears this call. So, is Druidry the indigenous spirituality of northwestern Europe? Well, yes and no...

❧ The Roots Run Deep ❧

The 17th century saw a revival of Druidry in the British Isles. These mostly Christian Druids were inspired, in part, by a growing curiosity about ancient stone monuments such as Stonehenge and Avebury. These megalithic structures were believed by the revivalists to be the work of the Druids. Although we now know that such structures are in fact pre-Celtic, they nevertheless remain an intriguing key to our pre-Christian heritage. The potential for these extraordinary stone circles, burial chambers and mounds to connect us in some way to the

knowledge and wisdom of the indigenous people of these lands is still relevant in Druidry today. Through these sites — and the land beneath our feet — we can sense a thread through time; a soul connection to those peoples who have gone before. The revival was perhaps searching for a Golden Age of lost wisdom — one heavily overlaid with Christian ideals — but it sowed the seed for what has become the diverse Druidry of today.

❧ The Celts ❧

Although many people are drawn to the current incarnation of the path because of a love of ancient Celtic culture, what we actually know about the spiritual practices of the Celts is limited. Classical authors, such as Julius Caesar and Pliny the Elder, recorded details of a people who performed human sacrifice — although the reliability of these sources has been debated. However, these accounts also made intriguing references to the Celtic reverence for sacred groves and their veneration of the spiritual powers of nature. We know that they offered beautiful votive objects to lakes and rivers and created stunning and complex art in gold, bronze, iron, stone and pottery, each alive with flowing designs that speak of an intimate relationship with the natural world and its interconnecting patterns and cycles.

What we know of the Druids themselves is that they were a class of Celtic society whose roles were that of priest, judge, advisor and teacher. Classical writers also mention other categories of Druid. These were the Vates, or Ovates, skilled in the arts of prophecy and reading omens, and Bards, who were the memory keepers of the tribe — a vital role in an oral culture where nothing was written down.

Once Christianity had become the dominant faith across Europe, elements of the oral culture of the Celts were recorded by Christian clerics. These documents preserved something of

the ancient laws of Ireland and the myths and stories from Ireland and Wales — albeit with a Christian flavour. They act like breadcrumbs, scattered but tantalizing clues to earlier beliefs and traditions. Christianity couldn't entirely eradicate the influence of Pagan culture, and so churches were often built at Pagan places of worship; Celtic goddesses or gods morphed into Christian saints and Christian feast days were adapted to times of significance in the Pagan calendar.

Whether we believe that Druid wisdom went underground with its remaining parts subtly woven into the Christian culture that usurped it, or that Druid wisdom in any meaningful form died out, the yearning to reach into an ancestral past to retrieve its wisdom remains potent.

In the 21st century, Druidry's yearning for an ancient knowledge that connects us to the past and enriches our present endures. Like its 17th century counterparts, modern Druidry still draws inspiration from the Celts but its taproot reaches even further into prehistory. Present day Druidry's fascination with Celtic culture provides an opening into a forest whose path leads to a more ancient place still. We feel a vibrant current running through all those prehistoric cultures — the stone circle, the tomb builders and the cave painters — right back to the dwellers of the primordial forests and the earliest human communities. Druidry suggests to us that the connection to the land that we sense our most ancient ancestors possessed still exists somewhere deep within us.

In our Druid practice, we tug on the thread that joins us to those first humans. We feel that shining cord woven into our DNA and we see it flowing through us and out into the future, in search of the hearts and souls yet to come. Our sense of this connecting current through time and place stirs in us a profound calling to examine our relationship with the land, with the planet and all beings. It challenges us to see that the thread is part of a web, a network of extraordinary beauty and complexity.

Sensing our place on the continuum, Druidry honours its ancient roots but recognizes that every spiritual tradition is a living, breathing entity that evolves over time. The tradition grows through the experiences and understanding of every practitioner. So how does Druidry express itself in our modern age?

❧ A Path Without Dogma ❧

It is often said that there are as many types of Druidry as there are Druids. Druidry is a path without dogma: there is no sacred text or list of rules to adhere to. Each Druid is required to take responsibility for their own beliefs and is encouraged to question and examine the beliefs and practices of Druidry.

Simple faith in a doctrine is not enough: the path must measure up to the individual's integrity and lived experience. In this way, a Druid's relationship with the path is constantly evolving and has led to a spirituality that is rich and varied in its expression.

Many used to a more prescribed path, might at first find the lack of dogma a little unsettling; they might assume that a path without rules lacks concrete guidance, or might exhibit a lack of shared values or cohesion. However, despite the freedom gifted by Druidry to craft a path unique to the needs of the individual, there are still core values that each Druid shares.

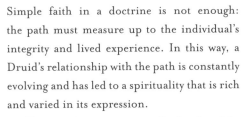

Druidry's Core Values

Druidry is an Earth-loving spirituality. It can help us to live more fully in our world and in greater harmony with all who share it. It takes its inspiration from the known wisdom of our ancestors, adapting it to modern sensibilities and expanding upon it in ways that honour the past and enrich the present. It gifts us with tools to foster a deeper connection to life, self and community; to come to a more profound understanding of our humanity and to grasp what it means to be a part of a wider ecosystem. It asks us to care deeply about the Earth and all its inhabitants; to protect it for the benefit of all species and future generations.

Druidry is a spirituality of the sacred landscape. Wherever a Druid resides in the world, wherever we visit, a primary aim of our practice is to connect with the land. Whether we find ourselves in the heart of a city, or in the wilderness; whether in the lush green of a forest, an arid desert or frozen tundra,

Druidry encourages us to display a respectful curiosity, opening to the landscape, its flora, fauna, topology, geology and its weather patterns and seasons. All of these features will combine to create what in Druidry is called the spirit of place. Druidry seeks to build a relationship with the spirit in the landscape, to observe it with mindful attention that we might know it more deeply and cultivate intimacy. Druidry chooses to recognize and honour that spirit as sacred, and therefore to cherish and protect it. We perceive ourselves as a part of the ecosystem of that place and aim to live in harmony with its network and systems.

Druidry is an embodied spirituality. It recognizes and celebrates that we are creatures of the Earth and encourages a full and joyful engagement with our sensual and physical selves. However, it also recognizes that those very senses, and our amazing bodies, are a gateway to the magical presence of Spirit. Within Druidry, Spirit is seen to inhabit and animate the universe. Druidry acknowledges levels of existence that appear beyond our five senses but are, in fact, extensions of them — realms of magic and mystery that infuse our world and are a part of both our spiritual and physical DNA. The Druid seeks to embrace both the material and the magical, seeing no separation between them.

Druidry is a healing and transformative spirituality. It fully acknowledges that life can be tough, that there is pain and challenge, as well as inspiration. Druidry's practices can help us to face with compassion the difficulties and ugliness, and to live more fully the joys, drawing meaning, wisdom and healing from the full spectrum of our experiences. Through its honouring of the rhythms and seasons of nature, and the cycles of life, death and rebirth, it offers the ability to work positively with change. Through explorations of the self, it is a transformative path that helps us to become more authentically ourselves.

Druidry is an ecological spirituality. Recognizing the interconnected and interdependent nature of life on Earth, Druidry understands the potential fragility of ecosystems and the detrimental impact that human beings are currently having on their delicate balance. It asks of us that we take personal responsibility for our part in the disruption of that balance and to seek out and implement — to the best of our ability — practical ways to help restore it. This might take the form of reviewing our current use of resources and energy and finding ways to limit or make it more efficient. We might reuse, refill and recycle; we might plant trees or support organizations that campaign and work towards a greener, more sustainable future.

Druidry is a creative spirituality. It celebrates our talents and supports the development of our gifts. It encourages a sharing of these with the world, understanding that we each have something of value to add to the unfolding story of life. The US psychologist Abraham Maslow recognized, through what he termed the "hierarchy of needs," that when humankind's most basic needs are met — once we have food, shelter and safety — we will endeavour to move towards self-realisation. Maslow understood that this drive to actualize our greatest potential is a fundamental part of our humanity. In other words, as long as we are not starving, homeless or war-torn — consumed wholly by the demands of mere survival — we will come to a point when the urge to express, create, grow and flourish will move in us.

Druidry shares Maslow's understanding that human beings are born to express our passions and gifts; creativity is inherently a part of our humanity. Druidry celebrates creativity as a sacred act and as something that promotes our personal wellbeing and benefits the health of our communities.

Druidry is an ethical spirituality. It encourages us to face social and environmental challenges with compassion and with a willingness to offer ourselves as agents of positive change. We cultivate a sense of fairness and justice in all our dealings and contribute to healing the injustices of our world. We strive for peaceful resolution amidst conflicts and think deeply about the impact of our actions on other beings, the wider world and ourselves.

Druidry not only recognizes the interdependence of the natural world, it sees our own social systems as an equally interconnected whole. The balance of this whole can be negatively impacted in much the same way that nature's ecosystems can be disrupted. A lack of social justice, equality and fairness can severely damage individuals and communities, creating dysfunctional societies that exploit and neglect the wellbeing of their members. Druidry explores ways of creating community that not only benefit humans but the natural world too. It calls for an economic framework that is sustainable for the planet, but one that also brings optimal wellbeing, health and prosperity for all. Druidry sees an important connection between the healthy functioning of human societies and the healthy balance of the Earth's systems.

❊ Look Back to Learn: ❊ Move Forward and Flourish

As we can see, Druidry is a spiritual path well suited to the challenges and sensibilities of our modern age. Druidry seeks the wisdom of our ancestors whilst also understanding that we, too, are the ancestors of our descendants; the choices and actions we make today will be our legacy to them. Now we have explored Druidry's core beliefs, let's see how these take shape in practice.

CHAPTER TWO

The Sacred Braid ~ Bard, Ovate and Druid

D ruid spirituality comprises three paths in one. The first of these is the way of the Bard, the second is that of the Ovate and the third is the path of the Druid. These are based on roles that ancient Druids performed in their communities. In modern Druidry, these are often referred to as grades. When studied they are distinct and separate disciplines, each with their own focus and practices; however, at a deeper level they act as an interwoven plait, each a worthy area of study but together offering a strength greater than their individual threads. Many will feel a natural affinity for one of the three paths — perhaps because it reflects particular talents and interests — but all three paths will be studied.

The Way of the Bard

The ancient Bards were the keepers of the genealogy of the tribe. In a society without written records, they were the storytellers and myth-keepers — human receptacles of ancestral wisdom, memorized and passed down from generation to generation. This rich oral tradition was vital to the health and integrity of the collective because it taught of the lessons learned and wisdom gained by the ancestors. Such precious knowledge, layered like strata of mulch in a forest, became the rich soil from which the tribe could continue to flourish. For ancient Bards, the spoken word was a powerful, magical substance, and the weaving together of words into story, prayer, blessing or curse was seen as a transformative act.

For modern Bards, the transformative power of creativity is no less important. We may no longer live in an oral culture, but we still understand the power of language to bring change for good or ill. As Bards we become mindful of the capacity of words to shape our thoughts and perceptions; our inner self-talk or the language we use towards others can empower or disempower, and so we learn to choose them carefully and wisely. For the Bard, words are magical agents of change.

Bards are magicians who conjure from the abstract world of concept. With creative effort, Bards transform thought and vision into matter. We learn to envision an intention clearly in our mind and with passion, action and focus craft this into being. We do this whether we are writing a book, baking a cake or creating a garden; the Bardic arts are not only those of music, art, poetry and storytelling, they are all acts of creation.

The way of the Bard reminds us that in expressing our creativity we are sharing something of what it means to be human. Even if we don't feel particularly gifted, we are still creative beings, each with our own stories to tell of how we might heal and transcend our sorrows; of how we might embrace and give thanks for our joys. A Gorsedd (*Gor-seth*) — a term for a gathering of Druids — will often include an Eisteddfod (*Eye-steth-vod*), which is the sharing of Bardic arts such as storytelling, poetry, music and song.

All creative and magical acts have consequences; the Bardic path requires us to think deeply and responsibly about our creations. It asks that we consider if they will be beneficial for ourselves and others. Will they heal or harm? Will they be a worthy gift to the collective knowledge and experience we are passing on to future generations?

Bardic skills are intimately connected to listening and speaking in their widest context. The Bard listens not only to the songs of human hearts but to the voices of nature, recognizing that all beings resonate with a unique frequency. A pebble on a beach, a mountain range, a stag on the heath, a tree in the forest: each possesses its own notes and rhythms that ripple out and join all the other sounds of nature in a vast tonal outpouring.

All beings, animate and inanimate, share a subtle energetic frequency. Part of the Bard's training is to tune into, and interpret, the individual voices we encounter in the natural world, letting these infuse our creativity, knowing that the passing on of collective wisdom is not limited to the human tribe. We do not only listen with our ears but with our hearts, instincts and intuitions. When we are closely attuned, we can hear every facet of nature express its story and its lived experience. In taking the time to hear and understand, we transcend our separateness and touch upon our commonality as members of the family of life.

The Way of the Ovate

The ancient Ovates were the seers and healers of the tribe, and this is still true for modern Ovates. The Ovate path takes us further into nature to find the hidden and darkest corners of the forest. It leads us deeper into self to discover the wildest reaches

of our inner landscape. Ovate training aims to heighten our sensitivity to nature's energies, its cycles and seasons, but also to the mysterious Otherworld that exists beyond the restrictions of time and place.

Ovates study the plant, animal and mineral kingdom, seeking to build relationships with them, learning of their healing qualities. They are often herbalists or energy healers, psychics and sensitives, acutely aware of the energetic world that shimmers and flows beneath the surface of things. Ovates have much in common with witches and shamans, understanding that the seemingly solid material world is actually a web of dancing particles. If the Bard hears and expresses the songs of nature, the Ovate sees and feels them as threads of energy, seeking to heal any break in those threads, or any blockage and disruption of the flow along their filaments.

Like the witch and shaman, Ovates have one foot in the mundane world and one in the world of spirit. They can be mediums and feel the presence of otherworldly beings or those departed from our world. They seek to understand the mysteries of death and rebirth and our place as the bridge between our ancestors and descendants.

The Ovate path can often involve a psychological journey to the Underworld. Such journeys are a theme in myths from many cultures and while, on the surface, they symbolize the seasonal cycles — explaining the lifeless winters and the return of spring — they are also important tales, which illuminate painful confrontations with our own shadow and our powerlessness and fear.

We might experience the Underworld when we encounter death, bereavement, illness or loss. Psychologically, such experiences can bring depression and a loss of meaning in their wake — familiar structures that have helped us navigate life can crumble, leaving us cut adrift. We might no longer know who we are. The Underworld is within us as individuals, and also as a collective. It is that which lies beyond the comfortable, known boundaries of the ego. In all Underworld journeys there is a sense that we must surrender to the process, dying to our old selves that we might be reborn. The Ovate learns to recognize this as a moment of transition: that something deep within is striving for a greater authenticity, a truer shape.

In experiencing such journeys themselves, Ovates learn a deeper compassion and empathy for the human condition. In coming to understand this process through personal experience — deeply and profoundly lived — the Ovate can connect to their capacity to heal themselves and help in the healing of others.

The Way of the Druid

The path of the Bard explores the experience of our humanity through creative self-expression. The path of the Ovate explores the deeper mysteries of nature, death and rebirth, and its healing wisdom. The path of the Druid ponders the deeper philosophical meanings of self, community and nature. It seeks to understand the relationships between these and how they might function in harmony for the highest good of all.

The ancient Druids were known to be judges, advisors and teachers; they were mediators of conflict and facilitators of public ritual. This ancient role as a person of wise counsel is the aim of today's Druids. We seek that part of ourselves that has learned wisdom through experience, contemplating the deeper philosophical meaning of our existence and how this might be applied in beneficial ways.

The way of the Druid is often the path of the counsellor. Whereas the Ovate might work more with subtle energy to heal, the Druid might turn to talking therapies, or methods that use self-exploration and self-knowledge as a road to transformation

(although deep inner work certainly has an Ovate feel to it too). Ideally, the modern Druid is a mediator, seeking peaceful resolution to conflict. "Know thyself" is a Druid adage. We perceive a link between self-knowledge and the wellbeing and development of the individual. We also recognize the connection between self-exploration and the health of the collective. The Druid understands that if every individual gains a deeper awareness of their issues, we stand a better chance of creating harmonious communities. Essentially the peace and healing that we seek to find in ourselves — learning to manage our inner conflict and destructive emotional tendencies — can lead to healthier, happier and more peaceful societies.

The Druid is often a campaigner, whether this be environmental activism, working for the humane treatment of animals, or challenging social and political injustice to create fairer societies. The Druid acknowledges that any injustice upsets the health and balance of the whole and seeks to remedy this as best they can.

Druids may feel drawn to teach Druidry, or to facilitate ritual or workshops. Druidry differs from some other spiritualities in that there are no clergy. Each Druid is their own priest or priestess, performing ceremonies and having direct contact with sacred forces in their practice. However, some individuals will excel at organizing events, or at writing and facilitating rituals for groups, others at conveying teachings — these become their gift of service to their communities. They might also perform as celebrants for important life rites such as weddings, funerals or baby naming ceremonies. Essentially, when we reach the path of the Druid, we look for ways in which we might serve our communities and nature with the knowledge we have gained.

❧ The End is the Beginning ❧

In completing the three grades, we find that the end is a beginning. Potentially, we never stop learning and growing through these three paths and can revisit each over time if we wish, discovering new insights and a deeper appreciation of their gifts.

CHAPTER THREE

Stepping into the Current ~ Nwyfre and Awen

Druid practice not only trains us to engage fully with our five senses, it also helps us to develop antennae for "unseen" energies. These forces can be felt at the edge of our physical senses and therefore might appear supernatural and "beyond" the material world, but, in truth, they flow within all of creation and are an extension of it.

Two such subtle energies with which Druids actively work to develop a connection are Nwyfre (*Nwoy-vre*) and Awen (*Ah-wen*).

Nwyfre

Nwyfre is sometimes defined as "life force". It is the vital force that flows through all living things. In Druidry, what constitutes "living" covers a spectrum that includes not only the human, animal and plant kingdoms but also the "mineral" world — the air, soil, sun, water, weather systems and the planet itself. Even in a body that has died — and is therefore technically devoid of Nwyfre — we can sense its energetic pulsing in the forces of decay, in the living bacteria and microbes that assist in the breaking down of tissue. Nwyfre is life in action — it is both the fuel and the motion.

Nwyfre is abundant and infinite and yet the flow of its energy can wax and wane, or even become blocked. We can best understand this when we examine the way Nwyfre works in our bodies. Many emotions and sensations surface within us daily. Ideally these emotions are felt and then move through and out of us. However, if they remain unprocessed (perhaps because they are painful to deal with) we might continue to store them in our bodies, especially our muscles. This might manifest as knots of tension: physical manifestations of a deeper psychological discomfort. These knots can limit the easy flow of Nwyfre in our systems.

We can feel stiffness in our bodies, thoughts and emotions that impact our energy levels and sense of wellbeing, wearing down our immune systems over time and leaving us vulnerable to illness. If we train ourselves to remain aware of our energy flow — to the way Nwyfre is moving through us — we can utilize tools and techniques to remedy any blockages and increase our life force.

As we build a greater intimacy with our physical selves, we develop the potential to truly listen to the body. Both pain and rigidity — or even pleasure and ease of movement — can tell us something important about our physical, emotional, mental and spiritual states; the more we listen, the more we recognize the interconnectedness of these parts of our being and how Nwyfre is impacting upon them.

Druidry teaches that our stores of Nwyfre can be increased or diminished. Our habitual actions and responses can affect its levels for better or worse, and so remaining mindful of how we think, feel and act is enormously helpful. Excessive stress and worry, inadequate sleep, poor nutrition, a lack of exercise, dehydration, unresolved feelings and conflict are just a few of the things that can drain our life force. Luckily, we can address this with Nwyfre-friendly habits:

- Regular contact with nature
- Relaxation, meditation and prayer
- Wholefoods that are rich in nutrients
- Regular exercise
- Good sleep
- Drinking enough water
- Breathwork
- Stretching
- Grounding
- Loving and stimulating contact with others
- Releasing stress and worry

All of these will help in building and sustaining our reserves of Nwyfre. In some — such as breathwork, exercising, being in nature and joyful interaction with loved ones — you will feel an immediate lift. Others — such as healthy changes to our diet — can have a powerful impact over time. All will benefit our energy levels with consistent application.

Let's try a couple of simple Nwyfre-boosting exercises. Using our breath and movement — mindfully stretching and releasing — can help clear physical and emotional channels, allowing the free movement of energy to flow through us, strengthening and energizing us.

Stand still with your eyes closed. Empty your lungs of air and then take a slow, deep breath, raising your arms from your sides up over your head, synchronizing the pinnacle of your breath to coincide with your hands coming together in prayer above your head, fully stretched. Hold your breath and extend the stretch. Reach for the sky and feel the full breath in your inflated chest. Now release your breath in one forceful out-breath and let your arms fall to your sides. Breathe normally. Repeat three times, allowing yourself to become utterly absorbed in the process. You may notice a sudden increase of energy.

Another simple exercise is standing (barefoot), sitting or lying on the ground outside. We do this calming exercise all the time as children, feeling our bodies connected and held by the Earth. This grounding and centring act can leave us feeling both peaceful and energized.

Awen

With focused awareness, we come to feel the reality of Nwyfre. Whether its flow is strong or depleted, it is an energy current that can be constantly felt. Awen is more elusive and often perceived as an unpredictable visitor — it roughly translates from the Welsh as "flowing spirit". Its Irish equivalent is Imbas.

It is a difficult concept to explain but easy to recognize when it blesses us with its presence. A simple way to describe Awen is as sudden inspiration — a change of perception that, although transitory, can have a lasting impact on our view of the world. Druidry actively seeks to open us to this vibrant energy, so that it might move more freely and frequently through us. We feel its touch when our awareness is heightened and a dull, grey world — in one surprising and unexpected instant — is cracked open and flooded by the sharpest of colours. Awen arrives like sunlight breaking through a canopy of trees. It is a skin-tingling moment when the Divine breaks through the veil of our distracted thinking, shining a spotlight on the magic of the world, reminding us of our blessings.

Awen is symbolized by three rays of light — an apt symbol as they express perfectly the moment our dulled vision is pierced by those shafts of inspiration: we are rent open, and the light pours in. In the glow of Awen, what a moment before had seemed merely two-dimensional is animated with a light that renews and gives depth to our vision and understanding.

One of the techniques used to honour and encourage an opening to Awen is the chanting of the word. Most Druid ceremonies or gatherings will include the Awen chant. It consists of the syllables Ah, Ooh and En, the same note for each, sung mindfully with slow, equal length. If many Druids are present, after singing three Awens, the chant will ripple out in swelling and cascading harmonies. It is a wonderful sound and the silence that follows feels alive. The power of chanting the Awen, with others or alone, is that it gifts us with a magical shift that breaks down our sense of separateness; in both the sound and the following silence, we touch upon the spirit that shines and vibrates within all things.

Druids will actively court Awen by spending time in nature, truly present and aware, opening their senses, breathing in the Nwyfre all around them and experiencing deeply that exchange between self and environment. They will also go into the deep, still silence within them during meditation, letting their minds touch that fertile void. Every ceremony, every festival, every connection to deity, every moment of choosing to see the sacred in the mundane and the holy in all things, helps to shape the Druid's being into a stronger conduit for the blissful energy of Awen.

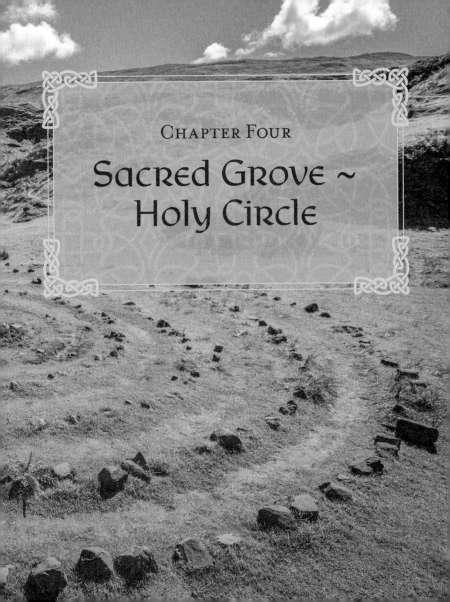

CHAPTER FOUR

Sacred Grove ~ Holy Circle

Within Druidry, there is no consecrated building set aside for worship. Druids see the whole of creation as sacred and can therefore perform ceremony in any place. We can meditate and perform rituals both outside in nature and inside our homes, or other venues.

However, for the performance of these practices, Druids will create a sacred circle with ritual actions. This helps to focus the minds of the participants. By creating a temporary boundary, we trigger a gear shift in consciousness, away from the day-to-day into a space of magical awareness.

The circle is the shape of sanctuary — a place without hierarchy, where all are valued and stand as equals. In the circle's enfolding embrace, each heart is open and accessible to all present. In three dimensions, the circle is a globe; on the deepest level, the ultimate sacred enclosure is the globe of our beautiful planet. Druids worship within the circle's boundary but we also understand its unending curve to be a symbol of the cycles of sun, moon and Earth.

If you were to picture the circle on a page, you would see a complex mandala that contained at its edges the four elements of earth, air, fire and water, and the four directions of north, east, south and west. You would also see the eight Druid festivals that mark the sun's cyclical journey and the eight monthly phases of the moon. There would be the times of the day, animals, plants and trees. There would also be the human life span and the full spectrum of human emotion and experience. In fact, all life can be contained in this spinning mandala: it is a vast tapestry of interwoven associations, relationships and cycles.

The circle is a wheel, constantly turning, bringing change. However, the wheel's hub remains still; the centre of the circle is a place that speaks of the eternity of each moment. Here we can paradoxically transcend change whilst also existing peacefully at its heart.

The Three Realms ~ Land, Sky and Sea

The three realms of Land, Sky and Sea are important in Celtic cosmology and we can include these in the visualization of our circle as a three-dimensional space. We might see this as the earth below, the sky above and the sea around us. Or we might link these with the Celtic realms of Annwn (*Ah-noon*), the Underworld and place of the ancestors (sea); Abred (*Ah-bred*), the Celtic Middleworld and the place of our earthly life (land); and Gwynfyd (*Gwin-vid*), the Upperworld and place of the Gods (sky). We might extend this vision to see them as places on the cosmic world tree, whose roots are in Annwn, with the trunk in Abred and the branches in Gwynfyd.

Opening and Closing Circle

There is no set liturgy in Druidry and so the structure and words used when opening and closing the circle vary. All ceremony can be adapted and the Druid approach to ritual is creative and flexible. The following is a simple solo version.

Entering the circle from the west, the Druid moves to the east, the place of the rising sun, to call on Spirit to bless the ceremony. Three Awens will be chanted and then the Call for Peace at each of the four directions involves moving to each point and saying:

At the North point,
May there be peace in the North
Then across to the South,
May there be peace in the South
Then West,
May there be peace in the West

And across to the East,
May there be peace in the East
Turn to the centre,
May there be peace throughout the whole world.

The Druid Prayer is spoken:

Grant, O Spirit, your protection,
and in protection, strength,
and in strength, understanding,
and in understanding, knowledge,
and in knowledge, the knowledge of justice,
and in the knowledge of justice, the love of it,
and in the love of it, the love of all existences,
and in the love of all existences,
the love of Spirit and all goodness.

Moving around the perimeter, the circle will be cast and sacred time declared. Walking the perimeter twice more, the area is cleansed using the four elements. This can be done once wafting incense and once sprinkling with water (incense contains the herbs or resins of earth, which are lit by fire and produce the scented smoke that is carried by air).

This ritual cleansing helps to clear the space and the mind of the participant of any mental, emotional or psychic clutter. When this is complete, starting in the east and moving clockwise, the spirits of the directions and elements — and their guardian animals — are welcomed into the circle and asked to bless the ceremony.

Traditionally, the animals associated with the directions are the hawk (east), the stag (south), the salmon (west) and the bear (north), but you could call in whatever animals speak to you of the elements in your environment. For instance, some Australian Druids will evoke animals unique to their landscape. Each direction is also associated with a season and time of day, both of which you can reference. The words you use are entirely up to you, but an example might be:

> *Guardians of the East, powers of Air, you are loved and honoured here!*
> *Please bless me with the clarity of dawn, the clear vision of the hawk;*
> *uplift my mind with your cleansing winds! I welcome you to my circle!*

Let your inner Bard create whatever words feel most appropriate and comfortable for you. After the opening, the main rite will take place. Ritual can be a festival celebration, or another rite. In Druidry, ritual is a specific series of symbolic actions and words performed with the intention of bringing about positive change, for instance, for healing or breaking a bad habit, or connecting with a deity, guide or the season.

The closing will acknowledge that sacred time is coming to an end and more Awens will be sung. The elements and directions will be thanked, and the circle closed in an anti-clockwise direction starting north.

The Four Elements

U nderstanding the four elements and their associations is an important foundational practice in Druidry, enriching not only our experience of them in wider life but also deepening our connection to their presence in ritual.

✿ Earth ✿

Direction: North
Element: Earth
Guardian Animal: Bear
Season: Winter
Time of Day: Midnight

Earth is the realm of germination, growth, decay, death and rebirth. Its spirit understands that there is a time for everything, that the laws of nature and the limitations of our earthly existence have their own important lessons to teach. We can feel this element beneath our feet in the strata of soil and rock, but we can also see its manifestation in the physical matter of our bodies.

Druidry teaches the importance of feeling the taproot of our body and psyche secure within the earth. This element reminds us that we are matter and to appreciate the value of gravity, the way it shapes and strengthens us. Earth asks that we slow down and relax into the moment. It encourages us to embrace the limitations and boundaries of earthly life and to recognize that inspirational flights of spirit must be grounded in the material realm to be fully beneficial. Through the slow pace of the earth element, we come to experience things truly in our very bones — in the movement and rhythm of our lives — and in doing so, move beyond the realm of concept to lived experience.

This element asks that we tend to our physical needs with food, water, shelter, exercise and cuddles. Through it we can ground ourselves in Mother Earth and our bodies, feeling our roots fed with the soil's denser, slower energy, allowing it to steady and strengthen us.

❧ Air ❧

Direction: East
Element: Air
Guardian Animal: Hawk
Season: Spring
Time of Day: Dawn

Air is intangible, unconfined, swift moving; it can't be seen but its presence is vital to our existence.

We can experience the spirit of air in the gentle breeze and the raging winds, but we feel it most intimately within the rhythm of our own breath.

The inhalation and exhalation of air keeps us alive, but this action can also symbolize the drawing in of inspiration in order to outwardly express our unique voice. Air is the vehicle of our self-expression; it carries our thoughts and ideas from the internal space of our mind out into the world through speech, the written word and other forms of creativity.

Air clears the stale and brings clarity; it is the realm of thought and intellectual concept. As oxygen feeds our brain matter, air stimulates our thoughts. It resides in the place of dawn and spring

on the circle and, like those times, instils a sense of lightness, freedom and hope. Just as our thoughts are unfettered by earthly restrictions, Air brings possibilities, ideas and visions.

❈ Fire ❈

Direction: South
Element: Fire
Guardian Animal: Stag
Season: Summer
Time of Day: Noon

We can see this element in the candle flame, the hearth fire, a raging inferno and the sun. In nature, fire can be both a destructive and transformative force. In some natural environments, fire can bring the necessary fertilising ash and heat that stimulates new growth. The spirit of fire is energising and warming, just like the fiery sun that fuels life on our planet.

The element of fire also resides in our own inner sun, aptly named the solar plexus. This area of the body contains our engine room, where we metabolize our food and energize our beings. Psychologically, fire encourages us to burn with passion and propels us to turn our thoughts into action, connecting us to our courage, teaching us that we can move through our fears and build confidence in the process.

❧ Water ❧

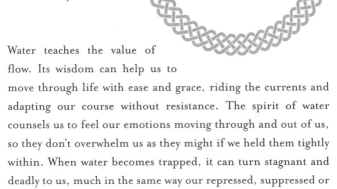

Direction: West
Element: Water
Guardian Animal:
Salmon
Season: Autumn
Time of Day: Dusk

Water teaches the value of
flow. Its wisdom can help us to
move through life with ease and grace, riding the currents and
adapting our course without resistance. The spirit of water
counsels us to feel our emotions moving through and out of us,
so they don't overwhelm us as they might if we held them tightly
within. When water becomes trapped, it can turn stagnant and
deadly to us, much in the same way our repressed, suppressed or
rigidly fixated emotions can cause us pain.

Our beings need flexibility for ease of movement; stiffening
on any level — be it physical, emotional, or mental — can increase
tension. To stay flexible, we need to keep moving. Water's flow
shifts us out of our stasis.

Water is the place of relationship and union — a place where we allow the connection with life to transform and heal us. It is reflective: we can see our image in its calm stillness; we can recognize our moods in its eddies and flows, our hidden inner life in its depths.

The Sacred Grove

There is not always a practical or appropriate time or place to cast a circle and call in the quarters. We might want to feel the enfolding joy and peace of the circle but not perform the full-blown ceremony; we might want to meditate or merely connect to our centre during moments of stress. Another foundation of Druid practice is the Sacred Grove.

The Sacred Grove is an inner space created in the Druid's imagination. It is known that ancient Druids worshipped in forest groves and that trees held sacred significance, so many inner groves will be a clearing in the forest. However, any landscape that holds deep meaning for you can work: a hollow in a sand dune on a beach, a meadow of flowers or a circle of trees in a valley — there are no limits to what your inner sacred space can be. The important thing to remember is that you are creating a sanctuary.

The Sacred Grove can also act as a starting place for inner journey work. These are meditations where we use our imagination to move through inner landscapes. These journeys might have a purpose, such as finding an answer to a problem, seeking guides and guardian spirits, or meeting with deities.

The consistent use of our Sacred Grove can be a powerfully supportive and healing practice. It is a place where we can silence the chatter of everyday life and listen deeply to the messages of our soul, where our intuition speaks and creative imagination is given life. We can approach it as our own personal portal to otherworldly wisdom and guidance — the heart space of our inner landscape.

❧ Create a Sacred Grove ❧

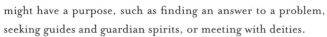

This is a practice that can slowly be developed over time. Approach it playfully but also with the reverence that a place of sanctity deserves.

First, settle yourself and close your eyes. Imagine a circle of light around you. Gradually see or sense the circle expand into a dome of light above and below you. Now picture the circle as a clearing in the forest — or whatever landscape you have chosen. Observe this place in as much detail as possible — the earth beneath you and the sky above.

Feel or see yourself sitting at the grove's centre. Visualize your heart with a globe of light surrounding it. Focus on this

light and gradually see it expanding, swelling out beyond you to encircle your body. See how this feels for a moment. Then keep expanding the globe of light until it reaches the edges of your grove. Feel your globe of light fully inhabiting the Sacred Grove; feel the peace, the sanctuary and belonging that this place brings

you. When you're ready, draw your globe of light back in. Let it surround your body, containing you with its soft and supporting glow. Open your eyes.

Once you have the basics of your Sacred Grove, each time you visit, enjoy imagining more of its detail. There will come a point when it appears as soon as you settle yourself. You will sometimes notice that new features appear by themselves, or you will encounter visits from animals, or plants growing that were not there before. Such spontaneous changes or unexpected visits often offer us the opportunity to learn something, to find solutions or to build a relationship with an animal, plant, tree, object or spirit being.

You may wish to use the Druid Peace Prayer when you access your Sacred Grove, or whenever you cast a circle:

> *Deep within the still centre of my being, may I find peace.*
> *Silently within the quiet of the grove, may I share peace.*
> *Gently within the greater circle of humankind,*
> *May I radiate peace.*

It's a beautiful statement that helps to calm, centre and ground before any spiritual work, or simply when we want to feel connected and present.

❧ Altars and Shrines ❧

Many Druids choose to create an altar in their homes. Altars and shrines hold a space for the sacred. We might have an altar room or we might only have space for a quiet corner where we can set up a table or shelf. Size is unimportant. We dedicate this space for ceremony, to connect with our deities, and to have quiet meditative time.

Building an altar engages our inner child because it is fun and creative. There are no rules — we can make it as simple or as complex as feels right for us. Many Druids will place on their altars items that they have found in nature, such as stones, shells or leaves; they might choose to have objects that represent the four elements of earth, air, fire and water, so this might be a fossil or crystal for earth, feathers and incense for air, shells or a small bowl of water and candles for fire. Many will also place statues of deities that they honour. Some will change the decoration of their shrine to reflect the changing seasons. Creating a place for mindful attention, to commune with self, nature and spirit — and to give thanks for the blessings in our lives — has a powerful magic all its own. These beautiful little spaces that we create with love open the temple door within us.

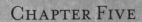

CHAPTER FIVE

Druid Festivals ~ The Dance of Sun, Earth and Moon

The Dance of Sun and Earth

There are eight seasonal festivals that Druids celebrate throughout the year. Four of these are astronomically determined points known as the Winter and Summer Solstices, and the Spring and Autumn Equinoxes.

Druidry has its own special names for these four festivals:

- The **Winter Solstice** is **Alban Arthan** (*Al-ban Arth-ann*)
- The **Spring Equinox** is **Alban Eilir** (*Al-ban Eh-lir*)
- The **Summer Solstice** is **Alban Hefin** (*Al-ban Heh-vin*)
- The **Autumn Equinox** is **Alban Elfed** (*Al-ban Elle-ved*)

The other four are known as the cross-quarter festivals:

- **Imbolc** (*Im-bolk*)
- **Beltane** (*Bell-tain*)
- **Lughnasadh** (*Loo-na-sa*)
- **Samhain** (*Sow-een*)

The cross-quarter festivals take place at roughly the midpoint between each solstice or equinox and were originally related to the pastoral and agricultural calendars.

Each festival happens around every six weeks and this cycle is often referred to as the Wheel of the Year. Marking each festival is a way of acknowledging the seasonal changes; it enables the Druid to ground themselves in the rhythms of the natural world, harmonizing with its cycles.

The festivals have seasonal themes and Druids seek to draw wisdom from these. Our lifespans have cycles too: there are times of rest, blossoming and harvest, of birth and death, and when we see these reflected in nature's seasons, we can draw strength from them and come to a better understanding of our own experiences.

To celebrate the festivals, many Druids will choose to gather in a group, known as a Grove. Some will feel happier celebrating alone. Larger Druid organizations will have their own rituals but there is no set liturgy and Druids are free to use whatever words, prayers or ritual gestures that feel right for them. Some will feel drawn to formal ceremony whilst others will be more spontaneous and flexible. Whether simple or complex, alone or with others, the important thing is that the Druid engages with the energies and themes of the festival in ways that bring meaning and joy.

Alban Arthan

21/22 December (Northern Hemisphere)
21/22 June (Southern Hemisphere)

We begin our journey in the dark stillness of winter at Alban Arthan. This is the season of the long night and the leafless tree. The cold seeps into our bones and life sleeps beneath the soil. This festival is the day of the longest night, but it is also a magical time of the sun's rebirth. From this time, the daylight will begin to lengthen slowly, heralding hope for the renewal of life. We celebrate this rebirth of the sun by opening our hearts to joy and optimism for these are a guiding light in the darkest winter night.

There is archaeological evidence in the UK that our prehistoric ancestors gathered from afar to hold lavish feasts at the Winter Solstice. They appear to have understood the magical importance of celebrating generosity and plenty at the leanest times of the year, and we still gather our "tribes" at Christmas (falling just after the solstice) — a festival that also celebrates the birth of light in a dark world.

We know that the worst of the winter is yet to come, and we must endure this, but the solstice sun is reborn and, with it, our hopes for growing light and warmth. In the depths of winter, summer plants its seed and the dark stillness explodes with starlight.

❧ Welcome the Rebirth ❧ of the Solstice Sun

You will need one large candle to represent the sun. Place this unlit in the centre of your circle or altar. Extinguish all the lights and sit quietly. Winter has come: the darkness has fallen. Feel it engulf you. Curl up in a foetal position on the floor and close your eyes. Allow yourself to feel your losses, sorrows and fears — the deep stillness of winter. Acknowledge all the feelings that arise but let them slip into the darkness. You are still and silent in the dark winter soil, waiting…

After some time, in your mind's eye, look above you. In the blackness, picture tiny dots of light appearing. Star after star begins to shine until the sky above you is dazzling. You suddenly see a beautiful shooting star streak across the sky. You know that this is your star of hope in the darkness, that its trail is a silver thread of guiding wisdom. Make a wish upon your star.

Remain aware of the glorious starlit sky but bring your attention back to earth, back to the depths of winter. With the vision of the stars still burning within you, open your eyes and light the sun candle. Focus both on the flame and on the periphery of your vision that is filled with darkness. Ponder on how this darkness can enclose and support you; it is not the place where hope dies, it is the fertile and mysterious void where hope is born. Out of darkness comes light and this is the simple but powerful message of Alban Arthan. Give thanks, extinguish the candle, relighting it each day.

Imbolc

1/2 February (Northern Hemisphere)
1/2 August (Southern Hemisphere)

With Imbolc comes the blossoming of the snowdrops and the first stirrings of spring. Imbolc is strongly associated with the Celtic goddess Brigid. She is a goddess of the fires of inspiration, hearth and forge, but also of healing wells and springs. At this time of year, we might see her as the sun that warms the soil. She comes to quicken the seeds of new life; to thaw all that is frozen and trapped within us. The melting of her healing waters cleanses the winter staleness of our spirits. She is the liberation of the land from winter's grip and frees us from our own stagnation.

Although winter is still with us, we sense the subtle renewing of life at the edge of our senses, visible in the growing light and the first greening shoots. Like a seed germinating in the dark soil, we, too, feel the bright spark of life that burns within us. Its call will soon drive us from the warmth and safety of the dark to the ever-quickening call of the light. For now, we must sit at Brigid's hearth, dreaming and drawing nourishment and comfort from it until the lighter, warmer days. At Imbolc we honour those dreams and the inner fire that will create the world anew — we, too, shall soon become the spring.

Snowdrops are the flowers of Imbolc. Their delicate green stems and white bell blossoms are a poignant message that new life is paradoxically both fragile and strong, vulnerable and resilient — just as we are. Life will always renew in its right and proper season; Imbolc reminds us to remain patient, to keep the flame lit, even if it is the dimmest glow beneath ash.

❧ Lighting the Imbolc ❧ Inner Fire

Settle yourself and close your eyes. Visualize a cold, crisp night in the hours before dawn. The twinkling darkness arches above you. You are sitting upon the earth. The soil is hard and frozen; the grass is glistening with frost; the land is silent and asleep. Your body and being are motionless, chilled and inert like the winter earth, but you sense an imminent change inside.

Draw your attention inward to the very core of yourself; this place is the centre of the sacred circle of your being, and it is here that you will light the sacred fire. This sacred fire is the fuelling heat at the centre of the planet; it is the burning sun at the heart of our galaxy. This is the fire of the smith that will magically melt and transform you; it is a candle flame of hope in the darkness. Standing at the centre of your inner sacred circle, you see the dry wood of your life, ready to be lit and, in its lighting, you know the heat will bring the first tender signs of renewal.

Become aware of your solar plexus. There is a flame that always burns here. In your imagination, take some of this perpetual flame upon your finger (it doesn't burn you) and now light the wood at the centre of your inner circle. At first it glows dimly.

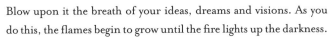

Blow upon it the breath of your ideas, dreams and visions. As you do this, the flames begin to grow until the fire lights up the darkness.

You find yourself back beneath the vast starry sky, upon the frozen earth, but now you are aware that there is a glow at the centre of your being. Feel its warmth and light spread out through your chest, down your pelvis into your legs and feet; feel it moving up through your shoulders, down your arms and into your hands and fingers, up through your neck and into your head, until your whole body is filled with its golden heat and light. You are radiant in the darkness. Stay here in this moment for a while — take note of the feelings and images that arise.

Your attention now moves to the land around you. You gaze down at the once-frozen soil beneath you. The frost has melted into life-giving moisture; droplets are hanging from the blades of grass, and through the earth a carpet of snowdrops rises, drinking in the life-giving melt, strengthening themselves in the warmth of your glow. As if by magic, you watch their brave green shoots pierce through; their delicate, white blossoms unfurl and hang in gentle bells of white. You have lit the fires of passion and inspiration and the land responds with the first tender signs of a new beginning. Pause for a moment — take note of all you feel and see.

When you're ready, gaze at the horizon. Along the line of the land, a slim strip of the sky begins to lighten: the dawn will soon be here... Finally, return to your body and the present moment.

Alban Eilir

21/22 March (Northern Hemisphere)
21/22 September (Southern Hemisphere)

At the Spring Equinox, nature is stretching awake and we, too, surface from our winter stillness, driven on by the growing light and warmth of the sun. Alban Eilir is the dawn of the year. It brings with it a sense of hope and the fresh possibilities of a new day. We see everywhere the vibrant spirit of the Earth, whose irrepressible life bursts forth in the opening of buds, the surfacing of shoots, and the golden blossoming of primrose, daffodil, broom and forsythia. All life must rise up from the dark soil and break out of the safety of womb and egg.

We give thanks for a rebirth of vitality and joy after the long winter months. We think about forging ahead and ask for the courage to expand beyond our safe boundaries — to crack the shell of our limitations that we might expand our engagement with life. We take action to plant seeds — both actual and metaphorical — recognizing that the struggle of the tender shoot

through the soil is rewarded by its blossoming and its fruit. We journey outwards towards summer, towards new experiences and lessons to learn.

At the Spring Equinox, the sun rises exactly due east and sets due west giving us a day and night of equal length. This balance between dark and light reminds us that Alban Eilir is not only the celebration of spring, but also a moment of equilibrium before moving onwards into the waxing energies of summer.

❧ Reaching for Balance ❧

You will need one black candle and one white. At the centre of your circle, light your candles and ponder on this moment of perfect balance between light and dark, day and night. Feel the equilibrium within you. Take time with this feeling.

Now turn to the East of your circle and say,

May I break the shell of my limitations of thought;

may my ideas nourish my being and guide my path.

Feel, see or sense the fresh breezes of spring blowing through you.

Turn to the South and say,

May I break the shell of my limitations of courage;

may my inner strength support me and move me along my path.

Feel, sense or see a vibrant sun in your solar plexus.

Turn to the West and say,

May I break the shell of my emotional limitations;

may my feelings be flexible and flowing bringing harmony to my path.

Feel, sense or see gentle spring showers washing you clean.

Turn to the North and say,

May I break the shell of my physical limitations;

may I be strong and healthy, manifesting with care the life I was born to lead.

Feel, sense or see a blossoming woodland full of spring flowers and the rising sap energising your body. Turn your focus back to your candles. Know this is a moment to take a breath before you finally make the courageous step to break free from your own shell and leave the winter behind.

Beltane

1 May (Northern Hemisphere)
1 November (Southern Hemisphere)

Beltane is the joyous time of leafing and blossoming. This festival celebrates sex and the transformation that comes when we open ourselves to another at the deepest level. This alchemy can also happen when we allow ourselves to be profoundly touched by nature. When we open to and merge with our environment, we can discover sacred union with the world itself.

Beltane helps us to recognize that life is a circuit that flows between our self and another, and, like the blossom that unfurls for the bee, in that exchange we are fertilized by life. Great things are born in us at such moments of union; this coming together of once-separate elements is where the taproot of our creativity feeds — without it we feel dry and disconnected.

Beltane encourages us to ask: "What is life without passion and connection?" It opens us to the extraordinary energy of our desire but also to the deeply empathetic nature of our being and

our ability to relate, make connections, and embrace our bliss. Beltane encourages us to feel blessed with a deep and abiding love — of self, others, and our planet — and through those healing fires of love and passion to find our true path to union within.

✺ The Nine-Flower Blessing ✺

Beltane is a festival of love and union — not only with the beloved but with the self. The following blessing celebrates who we are, joyfully praising our uniqueness whilst seeing our being reflected in the beautiful trees and plants around us.

In Welsh legend, Blodeuwedd, the flower maiden, was magically created from nine different flowers and trees: primrose, broom, meadowsweet, broad bean, cockle, nettle, chestnut, oak and hawthorn. These represent her power. Choose nine flowers or trees that you believe symbolize your most important strengths, talents and character traits. You will need nine bootlace ribbons of different colours to symbolize each flower.

Prior to the blessing, write down each of your chosen plants or trees in an appropriate statement that starts with "I am". (There are examples below.) Be as poetic as you like, the important thing is to celebrate who you are.

With your ribbons to hand, read out each statement, placing the corresponding ribbon before you until all nine are laid out.

Examples:

→ *I am abundant cow parsley that thrives on the margins (cream ribbon).*

→ *I am a courageous snowdrop, tender in the cold but resilient as oak (white ribbon).*

- *I am a graceful birch, grown anew from the scorched earth (light green ribbon).*
- *I am a vibrant poppy whose seeds of potential are many (red ribbon).*
- *I am alder, holding firm the riverbank when the floods of emotion flow (blue ribbon).*
- *I am herb robert, so often overlooked but beautifully formed (pink ribbon).*
- *I am the warm, sweet scent of gorse but my foliage is sharp (yellow ribbon).*
- *I am a sprig of yew: the wisdom of the shadow, the wisdom of experience (purple ribbon).*
- *I am a bright daisy and the child in me rejoices (orange ribbon).*

Take up three of your ribbons and braid them, then another three, then the final trio. Weave these three braids together into one large plait. As you do this, know that you are weaving the coloured maypole ribbons of your being into vibrant life and honouring all that you are. Focus on Blodeuwedd's vibrant energy filling you and your braids, saying,

I am life and beauty; I am passion and creativity.
I seed and bloom and fruit and seed again within the Greenwood of my life.

Keep your ribbon circlet on your altar as a reminder to celebrate yourself and the blessings of Beltane.

Alban Hefin

21/22 June (Northern Hemisphere)
21/22 December (Southern Hemisphere)

The Summer Solstice celebrates the height of the sun's passage across the sky, marking the longest day. We open to the sun's energy and inspiration as it warms the earth. Alban Hefin honours the sweetness and fulfilment in our lives. In nature there is an explosion of colour that can enrapture our senses. The sensual abundance of summer casts its spell and energy is high.

Counting one's blessings has a particular poignancy at this festival because, as we mark the longest day, we are reminded that

from this point the year will begin to wane and the days will gradually shorten. Transience is a reality for all of us and so we learn that our capacity for joy and happiness — like an inner sun — must radiate from within. It's worth taking a moment to ponder the mystery that at the height of summer winter plants its own seed.

Alban Hefin can remind us of the simple pleasure of being fully alive and present in the moment. The more gratefully aware we are of the blessings that enrich our lives, the happier we will feel.

❧ Greeting the Solstice Sun ❧

Wake before dawn and journey to a place where you can watch the Summer Solstice sunrise. Choose a location that is special to you, perhaps a high place that gives a good view of the horizon.

There is something magical about setting out in the pre-dawn quiet, watching the darkness gradually turn to grey. There is a timelessness about holding vigil until the horizon begins to burn, until the sky lightens into pastels and the landscape is washed in gold. Even if it is a cloudy day, watching the light grow with mindful gratitude, listening to the dawn chorus and seeing the world come to life can be profound and joyful.

You might like to write a list of all the things in your life that you are most thankful for and read this to the rising sun, knowing that without its glorious presence, none of these things would exist. Give thanks to our beautiful radiant star that gifts us with life, warmth and growth. Give thanks for your life.

Lughnasadh

1 Aug (Northern Hemisphere)
1 February (Southern Hemisphere)

At Lughnasadh we give thanks for the long easy days of light and warmth, the rich colours of nature's abundance and the first harvest of grain. We also offer gratitude for our own personal harvests — celebrating our achievements and assessing the results of our efforts.

The reaping and gathering of the corn and wheat grants us peace and prosperity but it also provides profound insights into sacrifice and death. With harvest comes the death of the corn, yet in the midst of that death we are fed and sustained. Lughnasadh honours the life that is sacrificed that we may continue to flourish and prosper. In this generous act, we recognize the importance of our gratitude; we learn the wisdom that, in its deepest sense, death serves the balance of life and delivers us the seeds of all future harvests to come. Lughnasadh asks that we acknowledge our food as sacred.

Harvest Blessing

Bake your own bread or find a nice organic loaf. Say the following blessing before you eat it:

This is the blessing of the Harvest.
The soil is sacred.
Food is sacred.
We are sacred.
We give thanks for the life cut down,
for its generous sacrifice,
that we might be nourished.

Break off a piece of the loaf and say:

Within me the life cut down is reborn. In the midst of death,
I am fed and sustained by the glowing seeds of new life.

Whilst eating, meditate on your gratitude for this gift.

❧ The Wheat and the Chaff ❧

As well as giving thanks for the harvest, we are given the opportunity to review our life over the last year.

In a notebook write the following questions:

➤ *What within me is seed?*

➤ *What within me is chaff?*

➤ *What is the blessing of my harvest?*

Take time with your answers. Make an honest assessment and take steps to release all that no longer serves you. Celebrate your achievements and give thanks for the lessons and the blessings of your year.

Alban Elfed

21/22 September (Northern Hemisphere)
21/22 March (Southern Hemisphere)

At the Autumn Equinox, as with the spring, we take this moment of equal day and night to focus on a point of balance. In the mellowness of early autumn, we can quietly observe this brief stillness. There is a certain relief in letting go of the hectic growth of summer. With the slowing that autumn brings comes a certain restfulness and acceptance.

Alban Elfed is the second harvest festival of the year, where we give thanks for the fruits of autumn. We also contemplate and prepare for our journey towards winter. As the growing darkness stretches out before us, we celebrate the paradox and mystery that in times of waning we are blessed with harvest, and that in endings there are fruits to nourish us through darker times.

❧ The Journey ❧ Inwards to the Source

This ritual can be performed outdoors on a beach, in a grove or garden. You will need to construct a large spiral of stones or pebbles upon the sand or ground. If this is not possible, the ritual could be adapted for indoor use, creating a mini-spiral with stones, cord or ribbon, or merely circling inward to the centre of your circle and back out again.

You will need a white and a black candle, a stone — one that comes from a place that is special to you and connects you to the Earth — and an apple to link you to the harvest.

Place a black candle at the centre of your spiral and a white candle at the beginning of the spiral on its outer edge. Stand at the beginning of the spiral. Have your apple and your special stone with you and say:

I ask for guidance as I begin my journey back to the centre of the spiral. I honour the teaching that this is the journey upriver to the source, one I will make many times in my life, as sure as the ebb and flow of tides, as vital as the in and out of my own breath.

Pick up the white candle and light it. The white candle represents the waxing energies of the year. Carrying your candle, your apple and stone, you walk the spiral, silently and slowly with focus and

intent to the centre. Take your time and concentrate. Feel yourself actually moving to the deep source within you. When you reach the centre, sit down. There you will find your black candle — this represents the waning energies of the year. Light it and place both candles next to each other with the apple and stone between them. Meditate on the balance that the candles represent; feel the light in equal balance to the dark. Reach for that equilibrium within you, sensing it as a moment of stillness and peace. Draw this feeling into yourself. Let it nourish and ground you.

Now focus on your stone. Imagine you have roots growing out of you, deep into the earth beneath you; feel it as home. Focus on your apple. Think of the abundance in your life, about the precious things within that you have brought to this place to nourish and support you through the coming months. Spend time with your feelings — acknowledge the images and sensations that come.

When you feel ready to start your journey out of the spiral say:

I have brought all that is precious here to store deep within me.
This place will nourish me through these coming weeks of growing darkness.
I draw strength to move on with joy and gratitude into winter.
I give thanks for my joys and sorrows, for the lessons they have taught me.
I welcome the letting go and trust in the wheel's turning.

Now slowly walk the spiral back out again… eat or gift your apple!

Samhain

31 Oct/1 November (Northern Hemisphere)
30 April/1 May (Southern Hemisphere)

Samhain is the festival of death. Nature is dying and letting go. In this process we honour the miraculous transformation of decomposition; the transmutation of organic matter into the rich compost that will feed new life. At Samhain, we also think about the ancestors and all our loved ones who have passed over. Samhain is a gateway, a door to be walked through. It teaches us that physical death and all the psychological deaths we encounter in life are thresholds between one state of existence and another. We can grasp the truth of this emotionally when we are confronted with endings. Of course, not all endings are unwelcome, sometimes they are joyous things: the end of pain or the close of a difficult time. Sometimes they bring almost unhealable grief: the death of those we love and the things we cherish. All endings bring us to that threshold, and to truly pass through it, we must surrender what was, to embrace the potential of what will be. The deepest mysteries of this festival are found in the profound change that comes at these moments of surrender. Our most challenging life experiences can soften into compassionate acceptance at that point of true release.

The inspiration of nature can help us deal with death and endings, gifting us with the courage to let go and the strength to carry on. The pain and uncertainty may be no easier to bear but the release of autumn asks that we trust in the process, bravely facing the growing darkness without ever knowing if the light will reappear.

❊ Letters to the Dead ❊

You will need a pen, paper, a candle and a heatproof container. You are going to write a letter to the dead. This could be addressed to a loved one who passed away, recently or in the past, or it could be to a dream or relationship that ended, or that which failed to come to fruition. Any ending that needs processing can be your subject.

Quiet yourself, close your eyes. Breathe deeply and slowly for a few minutes. When you're ready, begin. Write from your heart all that needs to be said. Take as long as necessary. If you need to break and come back to your letter later, do that. Be gentle with yourself as feelings of grief and loss may surface.

When you have completed your letter, light a candle to honour the person, dream or relationship and then read your letter to them. When that's done, fold your letter, light it with the candle and place it in the heatproof container. As you watch it burn, imagine that your words are being released and finding their way to your loved one, but also allow the transformative flame to help you let go gently with love and gratitude. If it feels appropriate, give thanks for that person, dream or relationship, and their blessings and lessons.

Coming to a place of acceptance takes its own time and grief must be fully felt and lived, but this exercise can help in that process, enabling us to feel compassion for our pain and to honour our loss as a sacred part of our humanity.

❊ Celebrating the Land ❊

These festivals grew out of lands with temperate climates. As Druidry has spread all over the planet, many Druids are now creating festivals that reflect their own climates and seasonal patterns. This diversity celebrates the living spirit of each land and brings richness and variety to the path. Explore the festivals in ways that deepen your connection to your own environment.

The Dance of Moon and Earth

The eight seasonal festivals and their themes can also be reflected in the monthly phases of the moon. The longest night of the Winter Solstice has resonance with the new or dark moon — that time of the month when it appears absent from the sky. The waxing crescent moon aligns with the energies of Imbolc. The half-light/half-dark first and last quarter moons reflect the Equinoxes. The waxing, egg-shaped gibbous moon corresponds to Beltane, and the waning gibbous to Lughnasadh, whilst the Summer Solstice resonates with the full moon.

Many Druids enjoy marking all eight phases. Some will work only with the new and full moons. Traditionally, waxing moon energies from the dark to the full moon are for creating, and waning energies from the full to the dark moon are for release. How — or indeed if – a Druid works with the moon's energies is up to the individual.

❄ Setting Intentions ❄ with the Moon

At the dark moon, or the waxing crescent moon, write on small strips of paper your intentions — anything you wish to achieve or make progress with over the next lunar month.

Place these in a special container on your altar. As you do this, imagine they are seeds being planted in the earth, germinating in the waxing lunar energies. On the full moon, take your intentions out of the container and burn them, imagining you are releasing them out into the world to manifest.

All through the lunar month, act in accord with your intentions; make small steps towards them and believe that they will manifest. I like to add a magical caveat to my intentions by saying, "This or something better; for the good of all, with harm to none." Our intentions might not always be appropriate for us and this allows space for the universe to present us with unexpected blessings.

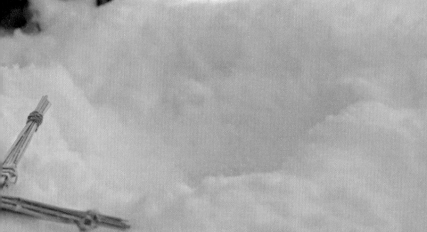

Ancient Shining Ones ~ Druid Theology

Each Druid is free to approach the divine in whatever way feels appropriate for them. In fact, you are not required to work with deities at all if this doesn't feel right for you. There are atheists who choose to approach Druidry as a philosophy and

feel no need to incorporate any form of deity into their practice. However, many are drawn to work with deities and there are a number of ways this can manifest.

Polytheism is the honouring of several goddesses and gods. These can be drawn from one specific pantheon or a mix of deities from different pantheons. For instance, some may work with only Irish or Welsh deities, or only those from Celtic Europe, or Scotland, whilst others might draw from a mix of these. Some will work with deities from non-Celtic cultures too. It's a very personal choice. There are **soft polytheists**, who view their pantheon as varied expressions of one overarching spiritual force, while others are **hard polytheists** viewing their deities as distinct and separate beings.

- **Monotheism** honours one overarching deity or great spirit.
- **Duotheism** honours a goddess and god – two complementary energies that are interconnected parts of a wider whole.
- **Pantheism** views the divine as immanent or an indwelling presence in the natural world and cosmos.

It is possible for a single Druid to work with the divine in all these ways at different times.

❧ The Divine Feminine ❧

Druidry offers us many faces of female deity to explore. Female images of the divine have been woefully lacking or suppressed for centuries in many places. In western culture, even if we haven't been raised in an Abrahamic faith, the assumption that God is male has become so deep-rooted that even the most secular of us might automatically think this. Seeing oneself reflected in the divine has been an immensely empowering experience for women in Druidry.

❦ The Divine Spectrum ❦

In attempting to differentiate the divine feminine from the divine masculine, it can be easy to slip into binary essentialism, assigning qualities to our deities that are perhaps distorted and limited by less progressive gender politics.

Druidry aims to be wholly inclusive — we all deserve to see ourselves reflected in images of the divine, however we identify. A Druid understanding of deity should ideally embrace a vast spectrum of gender identity. Druids from the LGBTQ+ community have begun this debate — one which can only serve to enrich the Druid perspective. Moving away from a traditional view of gender as binary — and seeing it instead as something fluid with multiple expressions — reflects the limitlessness of the divine.

As Druidry evolves and each individual Druid enriches the wider path with their own experiences and understanding, Druidry's perception of deity will continue to widen too. Druidry gives us the freedom to explore new lenses through which to view the divine and choose those faces that resonate most with our sexual, racial and cultural identities.

❧ Building a Relationship ❧
with the Divine

However we choose to work with the divine, the aim is to create a relationship with that force or being, an exchange of our energy with theirs. Like the best of human relationships, connections to deity are nurtured and grown over time with love and respect; this takes our commitment and dedication.

When we start out, we might choose to approach deities that appeal to us, honouring them with our time, focus and prayers; learning their myths and stories; meditating on their qualities and what these can teach us. In time, we might find that deities approach us. Many who have walked the path for years have tales of how a goddess unexpectedly turned up in their dreams, or references to a god would repeatedly appear in their life, acting as a prompt to explore further. This can happen when a

deity has something important to teach us about life and self. With experience we can come to recognize if the connection to a deity is "live", in which case we feel a powerful sense of their presence — a two-way flow of communication in those moments of synchronicity.

If we have a polytheistic practice, there will be deities that stay with us for life; we might also have deities that appear for moments in time, specifically to help with particular life lessons, then yet others that come and go and come again. If we approach deity as an energy that resides in all things, we might still be gifted with multiple expressions of that divine spirit. For instance, a lightning storm has a very different energy to a warm, sunny day, but both are expressions of the divine. In whatever manner we experience deity, there is no right or wrong way, as long as we act with respect and gratitude.

❧ Hybrid Paths ❧

The joy of Druidry is that it can be studied and practised alongside other paths. Druidry does not demand sole allegiance. You will find Christian, Buddhist, Hindu and Wiccan Druids — all of whom further enrich Druidry's experience of deity.

Some Popular Druid Deities

BRIGID (*Breed*) is one of the most dearly loved and widely honoured deities in Druidry. She was once worshipped throughout Ireland, the British Isles and parts of northwest Europe. Christianity made her a saint and Druids still honour her life as a saint, as well as her more ancient form.

She is a goddess of poetry, healing and smithcraft and is associated with the transformative flames of the forge, the nurturing hearth fire, the spark of inspiration in poetry, and the healing waters of wells and springs. Brigid's roles also extend beyond these, hinting at her ancient importance. She is particularly associated with the festival of Imbolc.

Brigid can be a fiery goddess who inspires and nurtures our creativity. At times, her fire can be intense and challenging as she reshapes us in the heat of her forge, but she also expresses a tender and gentle energy that heals our deepest wounds.

Brigid is passion and sun-bright inspiration, our heart-fire and healing peace — her precious spark of life travels within us from our hearts to our tongues in word and song, and when we see the sun sparkling on the ocean, we know that all life is born from her fire and water.

CAILLEACH (*Kai-yaik*) is found in both Scottish and Irish mythology, with traces of her making their way to England too. An ancient crone of the land, particularly of mountain, cliff, cave and windswept crag, Cailleach is also associated with lochs and bodies of water.

A giantess, her myths tell of her forming mountain ranges by dropping boulders from her apron. She is the wisdom of the ancient land, keen as beak and talon, the thrilling wildness of storms. The snow is her freshly washed plaid laid out across the land and she conjures the weather. Cailleach translate as "the veiled one", and in Scottish Gaelic "cailleach" is the word still used for old woman.

In Scotland, Cailleach is the goddess of winter who holds the maiden Bride (Brigid) captive over the dark, cold months. The release of Bride means spring can return to the land. In some myths, Cailleach and Bride are perceived as two sides of the same goddess, with Cailleach transforming into Bride in the spring.

Also known as the ancient Bone Mother, the frame upon which life takes shape, Cailleach is a crone of all-knowing. Rugged and timeless, she inspires journeys into the remote and lonely places of our souls. Her wild laughter is a sacred song of dark wisdom and maternal wit.

NEMETONA (*Ney-mey-tona*) is a Romano-British goddess. Her name roughly translates as "goddess of the Sacred Grove". Historically, very little is known of her but for a few inscriptions, however, many Druids view her as the personification of the Grove. Every time Druids cast circle and open to all that is holy within and around them, the peace that fills the space can be understood as her energy.

For some, she rules over our own personal aura — the subtle body that intangibly marks our boundaries. Her essence also resides in the sacred space of our hearts and the holy grove of our inner world. She is very much about our relationship with nature, what happens when we engage with the Earth in an intimate and sacred way.

We can call on her to centre and ground us with her serene energy. In connecting with her we can be called back to the present moment and find clarity and peace. She is the sacred relationship that Druids strive to build with their environment; she is the sacred relationship they strive to build with themselves.

CERNUNNOS (*Ker-noo-nos*) is the antlered god of the wild and lord of the animals. He gifts us with vitality and joy, connecting us with nature's powers of regeneration. He is often associated with the Green Man as the vibrant spirit of the wildwood whose energy is seen and felt in the bursting of seeds, the unfurling

of buds and blossoms, in the fruits of harvest and in the falling leaves. Like the stag that grows and sheds his antlers, Cernunnos moves through the seasonal changes, guiding us through the turning tides of our life.

He has both light and shadowed sides, like nature itself: he can be the heat of passion, the pain of yearning and the reverence that true intimacy and love inspires but he is also a god of the hunt — and of death and dying. This guise reflects death's service in keeping the balance of life. Cernunnos is both the hunter and the hunted and, with every death, he dies too, empathising with our fear and pain. In this way, he can also be perceived as a god of the grain and abundant harvest, who gives selflessly of his own body to feed us. Fearlessly facing death, with compassion and tenderness, he guides us upon a path of rebirth and renewal.

BRÂN features in both Irish and Welsh mythology as a king of Britain. Like Cailleach, he is a giant and possesses a magical cauldron that brings the dead to life. After being mortally wounded in a battle, he demanded that his friends decapitate him, but, remarkably, his head didn't decompose but continued to speak wisdom and prophecy. It's said his head was eventually buried at the White Mound — the site of the Tower of London — and that he remains there to this day, protecting the land.

Brân's name means "raven" and, in many ways, he can be seen as the carrion bird that picks the bone clean of all that is dead and useless in our lives; he is also the cauldron that renews our broken bodies and spirits. In continuing to speak wisdom after his death, he is the Otherworldly voice that guides us in our darkest moments of confusion. At those times, when meaning is lost, he urges trust in something greater. He is a powerful guardian and the voice of wisdom deep in the land.

CERRIDWEN (*Ker-rid-when*) is an incredibly important goddess in Druidry — her mythology plays a central role in Bardic training. The Welsh Cerridwen is the mother of twins — a lovable daughter and a challenging son. To gift the latter with traits that will overcome his disadvantages, Cerridwen brews a potent potion in her cauldron. However, the servant boy Gwion Bach, tasked with stirring the bubbling brew, is splashed by three boiling drops which he automatically places into his mouth to cool, accidently receiving the potion's magic.

Gwion immediately becomes all-knowing — and a chase ensues with a furious Cerridwen in pursuit. To escape her

wrath, Gwion changes into a hare but the goddess transforms into a greyhound. He, in turn, leaps into a river as a salmon but Cerridwen morphs into an otter. The boy then changes into a wren, but the goddess shape-shifts into a hawk. Finally, Gwion drops as a single seed into a pile of corn but wily Cerridwen becomes a black hen and eats the lot, consuming Gwion completely. Miraculously, nine months later, she gives birth to him and, placing the newborn in a bag within a coracle, she pushes him out on the ocean. Eventually, the baby is found in a salmon weir and through all these stages of magical initiation he has become Taliesin, he of the golden brow, the most gifted and famous of all Bards.

Cerridwen is a powerful goddess of initiation and transformation, deeply connected to Awen. She is both tomb and womb, midwife of the soul's journey, eternally reshaping us that we might make a better fit, that we might grasp a little more of the mystery of life. She heats what is raw in her cauldron, cooking it into a nourishing wisdom. She is the deep dark potion, the fathomless pool, where from the depths, transformation, inspiration and healing rises.

✺ Myth and ✺ Personal Gnosis

To deepen our connection with the gods, we can read their myths, examining the meaning of these stories and how they might relate to our lives, but a huge part of working with deity involves meeting them in nature and in the landscape of our own hearts and minds. No two Druids will share exactly the same experience of a deity, and no person can tell you who a deity really is or what they mean for you. You must find this for yourself.

Classical writers refer to the ancient Celtic belief in reincarnation, but modern Druids are free to come to their own conclusions about an afterlife. Many Druids favour the idea that we have many lives, not only as humans but potentially in other forms, such as animals and even trees or stones. This reflects an underlying sense in Druidry that any form that nature takes has equal value and meaning in the web of life.

Some might feel that the soul has an individual identity that remains after death and moves through successive lives. Others might view the soul as a collective essence from which we are shaped and where we will return after death — our individuality dissolving back into that essence, our lived experience becoming part of its evolution.

Whatever we come to believe, the Otherworld is a reality for Druids, a realm of existence that, although mostly "unseen", can be tangibly felt. The Otherworld is woven into ours, both realms acting as the warp and weft in life's fabric. The Otherworld is inhabited by spirit beings and deities, some with whom we will build relationships and others who remain mysteries to us — outside our understanding. Our inner world is intimately connected to this realm, and we can access it via our dreams and imagination. At times, it bleeds through into our material world, and we are offered glimpses of its beauty and magic.

This layer of existence is also the realm of the ancestors. Druidry teaches us a great love and respect for those who have gone before, and many Druids will create an ancestor shrine in their homes. The ancestors are perceived as great stores of wisdom and experience for us. They also remind us of our place in the family of life and of our responsibility to our descendants.

We Are All Related

Ancestry is not limited to our own bloodline, for we recognize that in our distant past, we all share common ancestors. Our work with the ancestors will usually be a combination of the following categories.

❧ Ancestors of Blood ❧

We inherit half our genes from our mother, the other half from our father, but, interestingly, not all of our ancestral heritage will show up in our genes. Our siblings might hold altogether different markers, and it is a mystery as to why we inherit some and not others. This poses some fascinating questions about ancestral connection, for although all our familial ancestors can be understood as ancestors of blood, we do not necessarily carry all their markers in our physical bodies. Despite this, when working with our blood ancestors, we sense that we are inheriting more than genetic markers; there is a layer of connection and experiences that resides on a deeper, perhaps soul level. For many of us this might bring great challenges and lessons — our ancestors were as complex and conflicted as we can be at times — and so blood ancestor work can demand compassion, understanding and an acceptance of the frailties and failings we are all subject to as humans.

❊ Ancestors of Place ❊

As well as family connections, we can also connect and honour the ancestors of the land that we live on. For some who have stayed in the same place for generations, the ancestors of blood and place are often the same. However, in a world where migration takes many from their ancestral lands, we might find ourselves in places with ancestors of a different culture or race from our own. It is important to acknowledge the ancestors of whatever place we find ourselves. We honour the indigenous ancestors of the land and also the many souls who have gathered there over time from other places, long before us.

❧ Ancestors of Spirit ❧

These ancestors might have no connection to our family or the land on which we live, but they are those who have gone before us and inspire, teach and guide us by their example. These are the ancestors of our soul tribe — those beings with whom we feel intimately in tune on a profound level. They might be connected in some way to our own life purpose and fill us with the inspiration we need to materialize our dreams. These beings will feel like kin — emotionally, intellectually, philosophically or spiritually — sometimes in ways that our blood ancestors don't.

✻ Connect with the Ancestors ✻
The Ancestor Necklace

You will need a length of red cord, three "hag stones" (these have a natural hole running through them, but you could also use stone or crystal beads), three black crow feathers and an apple.

Sit quietly before your altar. When ready, take the length of cord, hold it up and say:

This is the thread of life that connects me to all that once were, to all that are, and to those yet to come.

Take the three hag stones. These represent endurance and the cycles of birth, death and rebirth. Hold up the stones and say:

These stones are the strong and enduring links to all those that have gone before me and all those that follow after.

Take the three crow feathers. These represent ancestral knowledge and wisdom, the power of mystery, transformation and healing. Hold them up saying:

These feathers remind me that I am only the flap of a wing away from those I love and from those that guide and protect me in spirit.

Thread the cord through the first hag stone, looping and tying it securely. Thread the feather's quill into the knot to secure it next to the stone. Double knot if you need to. Now say:

This stone and feather links me to the love and wisdom of my ancestors. May I feel their gentle guiding presence; may their experience and knowledge bless my life. They are the roots of my tree.

Do the same with the second stone and feather, spaced out a little further along the thread. Then say:

This stone and feather links me to the love and wisdom of those present and those loved ones I have lost in my life. May our bonds be strong and nurturing; may the lessons we teach each other be treasured; may our memories be sweet. They are the trunk of my tree.

Secure the third stone and feather, again spaced out a little further along the thread. Then say:

This stone and feather links me to my descendants. May my living bless their lives; may they feel their roots deep within me; may my mistakes and lessons bring wisdom to them. May every cell in their body hold a memory of me and my loving support. They are the buds and leaves of my tree and they will blossom and fall many times after I am gone.

Now that the three stones and feathers have been secured, tie the two ends of the thread together to make a circle. Hold this up and say,

I tie the thread of life into a circle. This is the symbol of the eternal bonds of love and experience; the spiralling cycles of life, death and rebirth that make us one with each other and all creation. As this circle is joined and the knot is tied, I am blessed by these bonds.

Take the apple and slice across its middle so that the five-pointed star of seeds at its centre can be seen. Sit in silence, pondering on the mystery that out of death and loss, the seeds of new life come. Each one of us who lives, or has lived, or will live, is both the fruit that falls and the seed that starts the cycle all over again. Eat your apple and give thanks for this nourishment and the gift of your life.

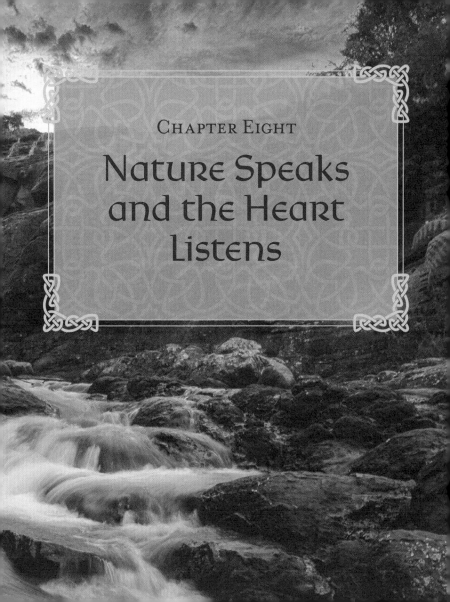

CHAPTER EIGHT

Nature Speaks and the Heart Listens

Nature communicates. It expresses its wisdom in every living moment and Druid practice hones our ability to be alert to its messages. Of course, it would be impossible to take in every piece of information from our environment — our perception is selective so as not to be overwhelming — but the trick is to be mindful. What we receive can simply be a moment of beauty or joy, but at times we might also find the answer to a problem or the guidance we are seeking. However, we are not merely receptacles for external signals; in Druidry, being mindful is only the starting point in a dialogue between our awareness and the natural world. Druid practice seeks to sharpen this awareness and keep the lines of communication open. It reminds us that when we allow ourselves to truly see, hear, taste, touch and smell, an exchange is happening: the object of our attention receives something of our own energy and being.

Druidry places a high value on building an intimate relationship with nature, spending time in it, connecting with its seasons, cycles and weather patterns. Our observations engender a deeper appreciation of the wonder these inspire. Druids seek to listen to the land and its sacred places. In Druidry, sites such as Stonehenge, Avebury or Chalice Well are perceived as special — they exude a tangible "something". These places possess an energy unique to that landscape but also the energy and expectations that people bring with them to such sites. When we

visit, at best, there is an exchange between the soul of the land and the soul of the person, a moment of true relationship. Such moments are when we stop being tourists — mere consumers of place — and connect more deeply.

If we believe in ley lines — energy networks that run through the land — we might speculate that converging lines meet at these most potent sites. However, as powerful and beautiful as these famous sites can be, Druidry teaches us that the entire landscape is sacred. We can discover sacred sites in the intimacy of our own locale, unknown and rarely visited places that we can return to again and again. The land outside is also the landscape within us. The illusion that we are separate from the natural world falls away as we build our own unique relationships with these special places; each, in its way, guiding us to the magical and sacred ground of our souls.

I remember encountering a poplar grove near a local river. After heavy rain the path to it was more like a tributary, making the passage through to the grove impossible. Even in dry weather the ground remained soft and yielding, but this partial access only added to the magical feel of the place. Like a tidal cave, the grove's waters would fill and recede. Opening and closing in this way, it seemed to pulse with the life of the river, with the rhythm of the grove's own inner nature, the core of its space a strange mixture of peace and danger. I was acutely aware that I must enter gently.

I was drawn back to this place again and again — and it soon struck me that the grove spoke so powerfully of that space within all of us that is harder to reach; those hidden, tender places with firmer boundaries, where the ground is more uncertain; a place we enter with care, our footfalls soft and sensitive to the ground beneath. That beautiful place taught me much about myself and my inner life.

❧ Seeking the Sacred ❧

Set aside a day when you can venture out into the landscape. It can be any landscape, even an urban one, but on this walk allow yourself to be quiet and receptive to the places you encounter. When we clear the chatter of daily life from our minds, we can begin to hear the landscape speak. The hairs on our neck might rise when we enter a certain place, or we might feel a sudden sense of peace and ease, or a discomfort and uncertainty. Examine these feelings. Are they your own or are they expressing something of the atmosphere of a place?

Choose a particular spot on your walk that draws you and then revisit several times. Begin to build a relationship with this

place. Take a notebook and jot down what you feel whilst you're there, any changes in the environment or how the weather and wildlife behave there. In your thoughts, greet this place with reverence and give thanks to it when you leave. You will begin to notice a magical change happen — your mindful attention, merging with that place, will bring insights and connect you in a meaningful way with the land.

❧ Animism ❧

Animism is a core belief of Druidry. In the Druid worldview, plants, animals, even stones, weather systems, rivers, mountains, and other "inanimate" objects are all in possession of a living spirit. Druids see the world inhabited by beings of root, bark and leaf; of seed, flower and fruit. There are beings of fur, feather and scale; of stone, mineral and crystal — each alive with a distinct spiritual essence, an innate intelligence and wisdom.

In the same way that we can build an intimate relationship with the land, we can also connect with the plant, animal and mineral kingdoms that inhabit it. Druids believe that we can hear nature's wise counsel through unexpected encounters with these three kingdoms. The trick is to remain alert to the possibility of these messages. When we choose to approach life with an expectation that we will be guided and supported, we become more finely attuned to when nature's voice breaks through, like a beam of light through clouds. These moments of inspiration and synchronicity often offer answers to a problem or prayer, acting as signposts or a comforting hand upon our shoulder. If we stay open, we often find certain animals, plants, trees or stones suddenly appear in our lives, or references to them repeatedly show up in some way. If this happens, I advise doing some research — I have often found that such visitors to our awareness offer invaluable lessons.

When we are blessed by synchronicity, we get that buzz of recognition, a sudden feeling of "rightness" about the message. When we are gifted with those magical and unexpected revelations, it is important to say a prayer of gratitude. Another way to connect with the animal, plant and mineral kingdoms is simply to quiet ourselves in our inner grove and ask which animals, trees, plants or stones wish to communicate.

When we are seeking to break free from old patterns and create new ones, we can turn to these beings to strengthen our resolve, or to deepen our understanding of the natural world, or simply to recognize them as fellow travellers on the path of life. Such an approach reminds us that all beings have value, that each can offer us insights that enrich our lives. Honour these companions as powerful teachers; recognize that there is a gift of exchange in the relationship and give thanks for their presence in your life.

❧ Druid as Forest Sage ❧

The etymology of the word Druid is believed to come from the Celtic word "dru", which means oak, and the Indo-European root "wid", to know. And so, the Druid might be seen as one who possesses "oak wisdom". However, for the modern Druid, this might more accurately be described as "forest wisdom", for trees are revered as great beings of deep knowledge. Ancient Druids were believed to worship in groves and modern Druids, if they can, will plant their own Sacred Groves for ceremony and gathering. For those not able to do this, many will perform rituals in the forest, or near trees in urban parks.

Not only do trees offer the gift of their extraordinary beauty, but they also play a vital part in the continuation of life on the planet. We can often forget the symbiotic relationship that we share with these magical beings: trees produce the oxygen that we

need to stay alive and the carbon dioxide we exhale is absorbed back into the trees in a continuous exchange. We breathe with the trees: the rhythm of inhalation and exhalation is like the beating of the planet's heart and, if ever we doubted that we were children of the Earth, than this simple, yet life-sustaining, act should easily remind us. There is in each of us, on some deep ancestral level, the memory of the primordial forest and our relationship with it.

❧ A Quick Note ❧ about Ogham

One of the tools modern Druids use to deepen their connections to trees is the Ogham alphabet — sometimes known as the Celtic tree alphabet — which has 25 characters that consist of various marks branching out from a central line. Each corresponds not just to a letter, but to the name of a specific tree. The alphabet also contains rich and complex layers of poetic associations. Its origins are unclear, and it is not entirely known if it is Celtic or pre-Celtic. The oldest surviving inscriptions are dated to the 5th and 6th centuries. There are also Irish texts from the 12th and 14th centuries, and a Scottish text from the 17th that reference it, but it was the poet Robert Graves, in 1948, who shone a light

on this arcane alphabet in his work *The White Goddess*. Graves has perhaps had the greatest influence on how people work with the alphabet today. He took the letters and devised his own tree calendar, aligning each Ogham tree with a calendar month. Although this is now understood to be a modern construction of Graves's making, many have drawn inspiration from his system. More research into the alphabet's ancient uses, however, will continue to widen our understanding.

Ogham can be used as a form of divination and self-exploration much in the same way as people currently use Runes. It's a vast subject of study and, if you wish to delve deeper, do seek out the suggestions in the resources section. There are Druids who choose not to work with Ogham because its 25 letters don't include all the trees they might encounter in any given environment. There are also Druids who find themselves in landscapes very different from the temperate climate of north-western Europe, and who are now creating Ogham associations based on the trees native to their own countries.

It is good to remind ourselves occasionally to be flexible in the systems we use. The important factor is that a chosen system should improve our knowledge of the natural world and help us to deepen our relationship with it, not confine us within its own dictates.

❧ Opening the ❧ Conversation

Learning about specific trees, animals or stones and building intimate relationships with them in your environment and on the inner planes of the imagination are key Druid practices. A starting place is simply to choose a being that you feel drawn to.

For a tree or plant, you might study their botanical details, researching any folklore or myths associated with them, and any healing properties that the leaves, berries or bark might possess. You may feel drawn to study specific animals, observing their attributes, or you might examine a simple quartz cluster you find on a beach or a granite outcrop on the moors, learning about how these were formed.

Having familiarized yourself, you could then spend time in quiet meditation with these beings out in nature or in your imagination. You might talk with them and take note of any impressions, feelings or images that come to mind as you listen for a reply.

Whatever being you are seeking to build a relationship with, approach them in the same reverential and respectful way as the landscape. Also, it is important that the relationship is reciprocal: if we receive wisdom and guidance, we must also give of ourselves. This could happen in any number of ways: leaving food for the birds; supporting wildlife or tree charities; doing our part to protect vulnerable habitats. Whatever can lead to the support and health of the beings you encounter will be a worthy offering. Also, remember to give thanks for all the blessings that these extraordinary beings bring to us.

Conclusion: Journeying Deeper into the Forest

Within a world where religious fundamentalism often brutally asserts the "one true way", Druidry is a haven of freedom and a shining example of unity in diversity. Its non-dogmatic stance makes it admirably tolerant of different approaches and offers everyone the chance to construct a practice that truly resonates for them. All spiritualities can benefit from regular self-examination — calling out any destructive approaches or blind spots — and Druidry understands the importance of this in its evolution and growth. It asks that we be confident enough to question the path, testing it for worthiness, whilst also remaining respectfully open to the wisdom of other practitioners' experiences. This is not to say that there are not moments when our highest values and ideals might slip — humans are complicated and we all bring our issues to any path we walk — but Druidry's focus on joyful creativity, its pursuit of wisdom and justice and its striving for compassionate inclusivity are all guiding lights when human frailty muddies the waters.

Druidry offers us a path that heals the split between spirit and matter; between our bodies, minds and emotions; between humanity and our extraordinary planet. It asks that we see our part in the whole, that we take responsibility but never lose our childlike joy and wonder at being alive. Druidry welcomes us back into the family of life, not as errant children of an angry parent god, but as thoughtful, questioning and aware beings, capable of caring action and positive change, of true relationship and connection.

Druidry's realm is vast, because its subject matter is life itself in all its stunning beauty and challenging complexity. Any individual subject matter in Druidry could fill volumes — its true richness and depth are difficult to capture in one book — but if you wish to go deeper into the forest, overleaf are some resources to explore as you begin your journey on this spiritual path...

Further Reading

DRUID ORDERS

The Order of Bards, Ovates and Druid: An international organisation with thousands of members, the OBOD facilitates an excellent distance learning course in several languages, plus events, ceremonies and gatherings. **www.druidry.org**

The British Druid Order: Facilitates a training programme, workshops, retreats and camps. **www.druidry.co.uk**

The Anglesey Order of Druids: Invoking and celebrating the importance of Anglesey as the chief seat of ancient British Druidry, this order facilitates an annual training programme, rituals, workshops and other events. **www.angleseydruidorder.co.uk**

Ár nDraíocht Féin: A Druid Fellowship (ADF): A Pagan church based on ancient Indo-European traditions, A Druid Fellowship offers public worship, study and fellowship. **www.ng.adf.org**

BOOKS

Billington, Penny *The Path of Druidry: Walking the Ancient Green Way* (Llewellyn, 2013)

Carr-Gomm, Philip *Druid Mysteries: Ancient Wisdom for the 21st Century* (Rider, 2002)

Carr-Gomm, Philip *What do Druids Believe?* (Granta, 2006)

Carr-Gomm, Philip *Druidcraft: The Magic of Wicca and Druidry* (Oak Tree Press, 2013)

Carr-Gomm, Philip *The Druid Way* (Thorsons, 1993)

van der Hoeven, Joanna *Pagan Portals — The Awen Alone: Walking the Path of the Solitary Druid* (Moon Books, 2014)

van der Hoeven, Joanna *The Crane Bag: A Druid's Guide to Ritual Tools and Practices* (Moon Books, 2017)

van der Hoeven, Joanna *Pagan Portals — Dancing with Nemetona: A Druid's Exploration of Sanctuary and Sacred Space* (Moon Books, 2014)

Hughes, Kristoffer *Natural Druidry* (Thoth, 2020)

Hughes, Kristoffer *From the Cauldron Born: Exploring the Magic of Welsh Legend & Lore* (Llewellyn, 2013)

Hughes, Kristoffer *Cerridwen: Celtic Goddess of Inspiration* (Llewellyn, 2021)

Restall Orr, Emma *Living Druidry: Magical Spirituality for the Wild Soul* (Piatkus, 2004)

Matthews, Caitlin *The Celtic Spirit: Daily Meditations for the Turning Year* (HarperSanFrancisco, 1999)

HISTORY

Hutton, Ronald *The Druids* (Hambledon Continuum, 2007)

Hutton, Ronald *Blood and Mistletoe: A History of the Druids in Britain* (Yale University Press, 2011)

DECKS

Carr-Gomm, Philip and Stephanie *Druidcraft Tarot* Illustration Will Worthington (Connections, 2004)

Carr-Gomm, Philip and Stephanie *Druid Animal Oracle* Illustration Will Worthington (Connections, 2008)

Carr-Gomm, Philip and Stephanie *Druid Plant Oracle* Illustration Will Worthington (Connections, 1994)

OGHAM AND TREES

Billington, Penny *The Wisdom of Birch, Oak and Yew: Connect to the Magic of Trees for Guidance and Transformation* (Llewellyn, 2015)

Billington, Penny *Nine Ways to Charm a Dryad: A Magical Adventure to Connect to the Spirit of Trees* (Llewellyn, 2022)

Blamires, Steve *Celtic Tree Mysteries: Secrets of the Ogham* (Llewellyn, 1998)

Murray, Lix and Colin *The Celtic Tree Oracle: A System of Divination* Illustrated by Vanessa Card (Rider & Co, 1988)

Matthews, John *The Green Man Tree Oracle* illustrated by Will Worthington (Connections, 2003)

MYTHS

Berresford Ellis, Peter *The Mammoth Book of Celtic Myths and Legends* (Robinson, 2003)

PODCASTS

DruidCast — The OBOD Podcast:
   www.druidry.org/resources/druidcast-the-obod-podcast

BLOGS

Philip Carr-Gomm: www.philipcarr-gomm.com/blog

Damh the Bard: www.Paganmusic.co.uk/blog

Down the Forest Path: www.downtheforestpath.com/about

Penny Billington: www.pennybillington.com/blog

A Druid Thurible: www.luckyloom1.wordpress.com